Scout, Pip & the Boy

by Scott Gibson, MSW, LCSW
illustrated by Rachel Dueck

There once was a boy.

The boy was kind and curious.

On the outside the boy looked very happy.

But on the inside the boy was very lonely.

Things happened to the boy when he was little that made him feel bad.

The boy didn't feel like he could tell anyone what happened.

The things that happened to the boy taught him things.

He learned not to get close to others.

He also learned that it wasn't safe to try new things.

One day the boy met a puppy named Scout.

Scout had a scruffy face and bright eyes.

Scout was young and ready for adventure.

Scout was also warm and safe.

From the beginning Scout loved to be close to the boy.

The boy and Scout became a pair.

Scout and the boy took walks.

Both of them enjoyed long ones.

The boy talked to Scout about his day and began to feel safe.

Scout was a smart puppy.

He loved to please the boy.

The boy taught Scout some tricks.

At night Scout curled up in a ball.

Scout leaned right next to the boy.

The boy started to feel safe and close.

One night the boy told Scout about the bad things that happened.

It was hard for the boy to tell the stories.

The boy cried while thinking about those bad things.

Scout listened to the boy and saw his tears.

Scout licked the boy's tears and curled closer to the boy.

The boy felt safe.

The boy began feeling good on the inside.

Others saw the boy playing with Scout.

It helped them feel good too.

Then one day Scout and the boy met a puppy named Pip.

She was very tiny.

Pip loved to play with Scout and the boy.

Pip was different than Scout.

She was very playful and loved trying new things.

Pip would climb on the table to see what the boy was eating.

Pip loved to play with the boy.

She often brought a toy to the boy to tug with.

They tugged a lot.

One day she saw a flock of geese and ran after them.

The geese flew away but the boy got scared.

It reminded him of the bad things.

The boy called for Pip.

He was scared that Pip would be hurt.

Pip saw the boy was afraid and came running back to the boy.

Pip licked the boy all over his face.

The boy didn't feel afraid.

The boy started to enjoy doing new things with Pip.

The boy taught Pip some of the tricks too.

Pip loved to go fast.

The boy learned that he loved to go fast too.

Others saw the boy running with Pip.

The boy smiled when running.

It helped the people smile too.

The boy went to shows with Scout and Pip doing the tricks.

People enjoyed watching Scout, Pip and the boy.

The boy enjoyed being himself and helping others.

About the Author(s)

Scott Gibson, MSW, LCSW has a clinical mental health private practice specializing in helping individuals heal from childhood trauma. For the past 30 plus years Scott has helped men and women individually, through groups and intensives recover the parts of themselves that were exiled. Scott and his wife, Becky live in the Chicago Northwest Suburbs and enjoy spending time with their three sons and families. Scott and Becky enjoy spending time training and competing in the many dog activities with Scout & Pip through the American Kennel Club (AKC).

Photo: Whitney Rupp

Scout—MACH5 Dogwoods Scout Out Loud MXB2 MJC2 PJD MXF TQX T2B2 NE FCAT THDX CGC TKN - Scout is a border terrier who loves agility and cuddling next to clients in Scott's office. Scout has titles in agility, Therapy Dog, Trick Dog, Fast CAT and Earthdog.

Pip—Otley's Pip Sweet to the Finish OA MXJ MJB MXF FCAT THDX CGC TKN- Pip is a border terrier who also loves agility, chasing geese and keeping Scott and Becky on their toes. Pip has titles in agility, Therapy Dog, Trick Dog, Fast Cat and Earthdog.

You can follow Scout & Pip and their AKC Dogstar adventures on Instagram @scout_and_pip.

About the Illustrator

Rachel Dueck (Rachel Joy Design) is a graphic designer and whimsical illustrator. She lives in Kansas City, Missouri and enjoys spending time with her husband Justin, daughter Delaney, and son Micah. You can follow her on Instagram @RachelDueck.

"We've known that dogs are man's best friend, but in *Scout, Pip and the Boy* we realize that our beloved pets are healers and life giving."

C. Bert Crossland, Ph.D.
Crossland Literacy

"*Scout, Pip and the Boy*, by my friend and colleague, Scott Gibson, describes the inner turmoil of a young boy and his pathway to self-discovery and healing from childhood trauma. The boy's inner world is entombed by secrecy and loneliness—until he meets Scout and, later, Pip. The love and acceptance provided by Scout and Pip transforms the boy from isolation and fear to participation and delight. Children who have experienced childhood trauma will benefit from the boy's journey of hope.

I highly recommend *Scout, Pip, and the Boy* for school counselors, teachers, parents, and individuals who work with children who have experienced the devastation of childhood trauma."

Christine Browning, Ph.D., LPC/MHSP, NCC
Professor of Counseling, Milligan University

"Scout and Pip are the 'heroes' in this true account of a boy seeking connection and safety. Due to the two pups' unconditional love, the young boy finds refuge and overcomes his fears to eventually be able to share his talents with others, leading to true happiness."

Kelly K. Olivero
Assistant Principal, Isaac Fox Elementary School
District 95, Lake Zurich, IL

"*Scout, Pip and the Boy* is a tender story about how deeply we need an empathetic witness in our pain. A licensed therapist and dog training expert, Scott Gibson reveals that our dogs not only keep us company, they hold our memories with playful, faithful care. In a trauma-filled world, we need this book...and our dogs."

Jay Stringer
Licensed Mental Health Therapist, Researcher, and Author of **Unwanted**

"Can our furry friends change and heal us? Author Scott Gibson gives us a resounding, 'Yes!' Read this lovely tale of a boy and his dogs again and again to your children and yourself; and be reminded that we all benefit from the warmth and acceptance that our four legged family members provide."

Steve Mesmer, LCPC

Printed in the USA
CPSIA information can be obtained
at www.ICGtesting.com
LVHW071336291023
762273LV00003B/5